W9-CPJ-763

3 4028 08488 0955
HARRIS COUNTY PUBLIC LIBRARY

J B Messi
Torres, John Albert
Soccer star Lionel Messi

$7.95
ocn840937671
06/23/2014

Soccer Star Lionel Messi

John Albert Torres

Speeding Star
Keep Boys Reading!

Copyright © 2014 by John Albert Torres.

Speeding Star, an imprint of Enslow Publishers, Inc.

All rights reserved.

No part of this book may be reproduced by any means without the written permission of the publisher.

Library of Congress Cataloging-in-Publication Data

    Torres, John Albert.
     Soccer star Lionel Messi / John Albert Torres.
      pages cm. — (Goal! Latin stars of soccer)
     Includes bibliographical references and index.
     Summary: "Read up on Lionel Messi, a soccer star from Argentina, who is considered
one of the best soccer players in the world. This sports biography covers everything from the
hardships Lionel faced when he was young to how he has become an international superstar with
Barcelona!"—Provided by publisher.
     ISBN 978-1-62285-221-5
     1. Messi, Lionel, 1987- —Juvenile literature. 2. Soccer players--Argentina—Biography—
Juvenile literature. 3. Soccer players—Spain—Barcelona—Juvenile literature. I. Title.
     GV942.7.M398T67 2014
     796.334092—dc23
     [B]

                      2013014030

Future Editions:
Paperback ISBN: 978-1-62285-110-2
EPUB ISBN: 978-1-62285-112-6
Single-User PDF ISBN: 978-1-62285-113-3
Multi-User PDF ISBN: 978-1-62285-165-2

Printed in the United States of America
112013 Bang Printing, Brainerd, Minn.
10 9 8 7 6 5 4 3 2 1

To Our Readers: We have done our best to make sure all Internet addresses in this book were active and appropriate when we went to press. However, the author and the Publisher have no control over, and assume no liability for, the material available on those Internet sites or on other Web sites they may link to. Any comments or suggestions can be sent by e-mail to comments@speedingstar.com or to the address below.

Speeding Star
Box 398, 40 Industrial Road
Berkeley Heights, NJ 07922
USA
www.speedingstar.com

✪ Enslow Publishers, Inc., is committed to printing our books on recycled paper. The paper in every book contains 10% to 30% post-consumer waste (PCW). The cover board on the outside of each book contains 100% PCW. Our goal is to do our part to help young people and the environment too!

Photo Credits: ©AP Images/Alberto Saiz, p. 24; ©AP Images/Alvaro Barrientos, p. 25; ©AP Images/ Damen Jackson via Triple Play New Media, p. 35; ©AP Images/Daniel Ochoa De Olza, p. 4; ©AP Images/Eduardo Di Baia, p. 8; ©AP Images/Emilio Morenatti, p. 40; ©AP Images/Fernando Vergara, p. 23; ©AP Images/Francesco Pecoraro, p. 32; ©AP Images/Israel Leal, p. 43; ©AP Images/Keystone/ Walter Bieri, p. 36; ©AP Images/Luca Bruno, p. 33; ©AP Images/Manu Fernandez, pp. 7, 13, 27, 28, 31; ©AP Images/Natacha Pisarenko, p. 20; ©AP Images/Paul White, p. 11; ©AP Images/Ricardo Mazalan, p. 14; ©AP Images/Ronald Wittek/picture-alliance/dpa, p. 17; ©AP Images/Shuji Kajiyama, p. 19.

Cover Photo: ©AP Images/Julian Rojas

CONTENTS

As the ball falls back to the ground, Messi winds up to take a powerful kick, then blasts the ball past the goalkeeper.

A Great Moment

Big-time soccer fans already knew about the player known as "the flea."

Lionel Messi, or the flea, had been a teenage prodigy and member of Argentina's World Cup team. But after this night, after the April 18, 2007 game between Barcelona and Getafe in the Spanish Premier League (known as La Liga), most sports fans around the world would learn the name Lionel Messi.

Messi was already known as a great goal-scorer and for an attacking style that reminded others of the all-time great players that came before. But what he did that night on the pitch would become the stuff of legend.

It was a clear, chilly night. Spring had not quite arrived in Barcelona, and the thousands of fans who packed the stadium wore jackets and sweatshirts to keep warm. This was an important game between rivals. It was a semifinal match in the annual Copa del Rey soccer tournament. Copa del Rey is Spanish for "the King's Cup." The tournament determines the Spanish La Liga champion for that particular year.

Messi, a striker for FC Barcelona, took a pass from a midfielder on the Barcelona half of the field near the far sideline. The nineteen-year-old, with shoulder-length black hair, then swept his right foot over the ball, grazing it just enough to put the ball on his left foot and avoid the first Getafe defender who went flying past him.

Another defender came charging from midfield, and again, Messi tapped the ball from right to left and evaded the Getafe player.

The score was already 1–0 in favor of Barcelona midway through the first half. Messi looked up and saw that he had room to run. With a burst of speed, Messi pumped his arms and legs, and roared forward while being chased by the two players he already avoided. He accelerated, gaining speed with every step.

But it looked as if he was running directly toward another Getafe defender. Just before reaching him, Messi again shifted the ball and his body to the left, sideswiping the defender and avoiding a slide tackle from one of the players chasing him. As he moved left, another yellow jersey was in his way.

Somehow, Messi was able to get the ball back to his right foot and change direction in an instant while still running full speed. That left another Getafe player shaking his head.

Looking up now, Messi could see only one player in between the ball and the goal. But this player was wearing white. It was Getafe's goalkeeper. He had come way out from the net and slid toward the ball hoping to kick it away, or at least force Messi to change directions once more.

It worked. Sort of. Messi had to shift again and tap the ball to his right, just out of reach of the keeper's

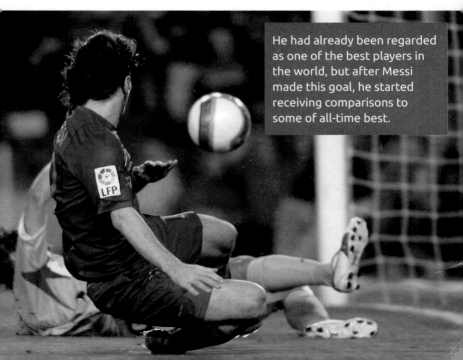

He had already been regarded as one of the best players in the world, but after Messi made this goal, he started receiving comparisons to some of all-time best.

outstretched leg. Now no one was guarding the goal, but Messi had tapped the ball a little too strongly. Now the ball seemed to be getting away from him as it was rolling hopelessly toward the edge of the field where it might go out of bounds.

But once again, Messi showed his quickness and speed, catching up to the ball a few yards from the end of the field. Then in one movement, he struck hard with his right foot at the rolling ball and sent a shot just high enough to clear

Messi became the best by learning from the best. His coach, Diego Maradona, is considered the all-time greatest Argentinean player.

one last sliding Getafe defender. The ball sailed into the back of the net on the far side of the goal.

It was an almost impossible angle, yet Messi, the scoring machine, had done it again. He ran to the corner of the field to celebrate and was instantly mobbed by his teammates. Fans rose to their feet and started waving white handkerchiefs and small Barcelona flags.

Messi looked almost overwhelmed while fans and teammates continued to celebrate for several minutes. It was one of the most amazing goals in soccer history. Messi had run more than half the length of the field, dodged and juked his way past five defenders who were attacking him from all different types of angles. He then skirted past the goalkeeper before launching an improbable shot.

Replays of the Messi "solo" goal would be aired on every sports television channel for days to come. Now everyone knew who Lionel Messi was.

Immediately, people started making comparisons to another famous "solo" goal by a soccer legend by the name of Diego Maradona. Maradona was known for having the "Goal of the Century" when he dashed past several players and scored against England during the 1986 World Cup.

Maradona's stage was bigger, but Messi's goal was just as impressive. It was fitting that Messi was compared with Maradona, who he admired as a kid growing up in Argentina. Those childhood days were filled playing soccer and dreaming of scoring a goal like he one day would.

chapter 2

Growing Up

Lionel Andrés Messi was born on June 24, 1987 in the city of Rosario, Argentina. Rosario is a big city located almost two hundred miles northwest of the capital city of Buenos Aires. Argentina is a South American country. The city has a deepwater port that connects with the Panama River and also has a main railroad terminal. Naturally, Rosario is a main shipping center for all types of goods that are imported and exported throughout the region.

It is a very old and busy city, rich in history. You don't have to travel very far to find a historic site, museum, statue, or monument. It was also known for its industry, and there were lots of factories around as well.

While his club team, Barcelona, is based in Spain, he stays faithful to his home country by playing for Argentina's national team.

Messi's father, Jorge Horacio Messi worked long, hard hours as a steelworker in one of the city's numerous factories. His mother, Celia María Cuccittini, worked part-time cleaning people's houses when she wasn't looking after Lionel and his older brothers, Rodrigo and Matías, and his sister, María Sol.

Because his parents worked so hard, Messi and his family were able to live in a decent part of the city. It wasn't the greatest neighborhood, but it was filled with families who looked out for each other's children. As long as you stayed in the neighborhood, you were safe. Messi's mother never had to worry about him.

"We lived in a nice, ordinary house in a neighborhood in the south of the city called Barrio Las Heras. It's still my barrio," Messi told author Tom Watt for a book he was writing about some of the world's best soccer players. He added that the house still belongs to the family.

"I always go home to visit when I can and still see lots of the same friends."

Soccer, or fútbol as it is known in Latin American countries, is the most popular sport in Argentina and throughout South America. Some of Messi's earliest memories are of watching his older brothers and cousins—who lived nearby—play soccer.

There were no fields, or pitches, nearby and so they would often play in the street outside their home. Messi was too young to join in but would watch and sometimes beg and cry when they didn't let him join. They were afraid

With his swift and agile moves, most of Messi's opponents are left with "broken ankles." This is when the person falls down because they can't react to the quick change of direction.

he would get hurt because they were often playing against older boys themselves.

The only thing Messi ever wanted as a child was his very own soccer ball. It was the first gift he can remember getting.

After that, it became the only present he ever asked for. It didn't matter how many soccer balls he had, Messi always wanted another. It was the present he asked his parents for every Christmas, every birthday, or any other day where presents might be exchanged.

The funny thing is that Messi never took them outside to play! He simply wanted to collect them. He was afraid that they might get ruined if he played with them.

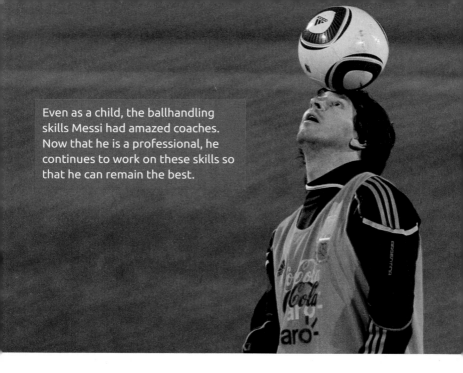

Even as a child, the ballhandling skills Messi had amazed coaches. Now that he is a professional, he continues to work on these skills so that he can remain the best.

It wasn't long, however, before the young boy changed his mind. He was five years old when he first ventured outside with his very own soccer ball.

"I didn't want to take them out in the street in case they burst or got damaged," he told Tom Watt for his book. "After a while, though, I started taking them outside and actually playing (soccer) with them."

A soccer field is called a pitch. There were no pitches to play on in Messi's working-class neighborhood, but there was always a game to be found. Many times the children from that community would be right outside in the street, playing a game. The roads were not paved; they were dirt roads. It was better to play on a dirt road than on a paved road. It didn't hurt as much if you fell down and the soccer balls would not get chewed up by the road.

Sometimes, when there were enough neighborhood kids to play a real game, the kids would sneak into an old abandoned army base in town. The base was known as the "Batallón." Messi and his friends found a small hole in the fence that surrounded the old base, and they would carefully climb through and then spend hours playing on the wide-open grassy fields.

It was on those grassy fields on the army base that Messi discovered something wonderful. From a very early age, he had an amazing ability to keep the ball away from the other players. They would try and try, and still he was able to dribble the ball in and around anyone he wanted to.

His older brothers were afraid that these incredible ballhandling skills would make other boys jealous and angry. They often watched out for him to make sure no one tried to hurt him.

"I don't really remember that, but it's what my brothers have told me since," Messi said.

They wouldn't have to watch out for him for too long. Pretty soon, the little five-year-old with the great ballhandling skills would start amazing just about everyone who watched him play.

chapter 3

Club Team

In countries like Argentina, soccer is almost as important as school and jobs. Soccer is like life.

There was a tradition around the Messi household and actually in just about every soccer family home throughout the area. The Messi clan was involved in club soccer. This meant that every male member of the family was expected to play soccer for Grandoli, the local club.

This soccer club wasn't just for children. Adults played too, including Messi's uncle who played on a senior team. So, as soon as Messi decided it was OK to use the soccer balls he had been "saving" and started playing with his

While Messi's play on the field has made people forget about his lack of height, it's hard not to notice it when he is next to his former teammate Ronaldinho.

friends, his family planned on signing him up for his first club team.

"It wasn't just me. The whole family was involved at the club; all of us played there at different age levels, and my dad was one of the coaches," Messi said in an interview. "We used to spend the whole day of Sunday at Grandoli because we would have a member of the family playing in every different age category, from me through to my uncle in the senior team. We'd be there all day."

It was 1991 when Salvador Aparicio, a well-known old coach with Grandoli, first noticed Messi on the pitch. He was messing around with the ball, just kind of playing by himself. Aparicio needed one more boy to be able to have a seven-on-seven game. It was nothing official, just a friendly practice game.

He asked Messi's mother if her boy would be able to play the game, but she said no. Messi was smaller than all the other boys, and she was worried that he would get hurt. Luckily, Messi's grandmother was there and she urged the boy's mother to let him play.

"Without my grandmother, I wouldn't have been able to start playing so young," Messi told *The Independent* newspaper in 2008.

Aparicio had coached thousands of soccer players over the years. But what he saw that day changed everything for him.

"The play went on and the ball came to him," Aparicio said during a televised interview in 2008. "The ball rolled

Because he has such great ball control, Messi has the ability to move the ball in ways his opponents cannot defend.

toward him and basically hit his left leg. Then he controlled the ball and started running across the pitch. He dribbled past anyone crossing his path and I was screaming 'shoot, shoot,' but he was too small to do it. Since then, he was always part of my team."

Aparicio knew from that moment that Messi was destined to become a very special soccer player. He would do things on the pitch that Aparicio had never seen before. One example of how Messi played was that he would never wait for the other team's goalkeeper to kick the ball once he placed it on the ground.

Messi would dart forward with blazing speed and take the ball away from the keeper.

"He would score six or seven goals every match," Aparicio said. "He was supernatural."

Messi was put on the most talented and most competitive team for six-year-olds because he was so talented. It was a team that regularly produced players that went on to play for Argentina's national team. There were other coaches—in addition to Aparicio—who were involved in teaching Messi the game.

They've all said that one of the main things that set him apart was that he really wanted to learn. He was a quiet boy and never disruptive during practice time. He truly took

No matter where his team is playing, Messi fans travel the world to watch him. This sign held by his Argentinean fans reads: "Messi we believe in you!"

the time to listen to his coaches and try to do everything they said.

Messi's ballhandling skills became so amazing that he would sometimes go onto the field and perform his "tricks" in front of the crowded stands waiting for the professional teams to take the field. Because he was so young—and so small—some people thought they were being entertained by a circus dwarf.

They gave him the nickname "Enano" which is Spanish for dwarf. Other people nicknamed him "the flea" because he was often the smallest player on his team.

But Messi and his family never worried about his height. They felt he would surely grow when he got older. All he cared about now was soccer. He loved it, he lived it, and he breathed it. He spent every waking minute thinking about it.

"I'd go to school, come home, and straightaway, go out with a ball," he told Tom Watt for his book. "Then I might go to training at Grandoli, come home, have something to eat and then be back out in the street again. I was always out in the street and always playing (soccer). I even kept a ball with me when I was indoors. My brothers didn't have to worry anymore: the other kids in the neighborhood sort of looked after me."

It seemed as if everything was going Messi's way. Clearly, he was a budding soccer superstar in the making. But a visit to the doctor a few years later would throw his family's world into a spin.

Bad News

Messi was a star player as a youngster for his club team, nicknamed Newell's Old Boys. But once players reached the age of thirteen—if they were good enough— the boys were expected to go try out for the next level of the team.

The team, River Plate, was based in Buenos Aires, and Messi would have to go to school there and live there away from his family. No one seemed overly concerned that Messi was still so much shorter than the other boys his age.

When he turned thirteen, Messi stood only 4-feet 8-inches tall. There was no doubt that he was good enough to play for River Plate, a team that would probably lead him

Lionel is shown stretching before practice for the Argentina Under-20 national team that won the bronze at the 2005 South American Youth Championship in Colombia.

to play for the junior national team. But when Messi went to see a doctor for a routine physical that all players went through, they found something that didn't seem right.

The doctor asked to see Messi again, but this time with his father. The team's doctor did not like what he saw on certain tests and suggested that the boy and his father go and see a specialist called an endocrinologist. So, on January 31, 1997, Messi and his father went to see the doctor.

The doctor gave them the bad news: Messi was suffering from a growth-hormone deficit. This meant there was something wrong with the hormones that controlled his height. It was also called a mild form of "dwarfism." Now, the old nickname didn't seem so funny anymore.

He may be shorter than most players, but Messi's skills make him the bigges threat on the field.

onel Messi is a scoring machine. His bility to jump much higher than his pponents makes scoring that much asier.

But the doctor could not treat Messi without knowing just how serious his condition was. He ordered medical tests that would take almost a full year to complete. The family waited out the year nervously hoping that something could be done. There was no way Messi would be able to have a future as an adult soccer player if he had already stopped growing.

After that year, the family finally received some good news. Messi's condition could be treated. The fourteen-year-old boy would have to inject himself every single day with a biosynthetic growth hormone.

Messi did not mind the medicine at all. After a while it became part of his routine, like taking a shower or combing his hair.

"It was like cleaning my teeth," Messi told *The Independent* newspaper. "In the beginning, when people saw me doing my injections, they asked what was going on. But they eventually got used to it. It wasn't really a chore, and I knew it was important for my future. And I was responsible."

Messi would later say that the main reason he was so responsible about his injection was because his future as a soccer player depended on it.

There was one more problem, however, that the family would have to deal with: the cost. The medications were very expensive. At first, Messi's father was able to pay for the medication with help from the government and the company he worked for.

But only a few months after the budding soccer star started his treatments, the world's economy began to crumble. Many countries began to have problems paying back loans and providing the services that its citizens were used to.

The medicine cost about $1,500 every month.

Messi's family felt that the soccer club, Newell's Old Boys, should pay for the treatment. The club sent some money but could not afford it either. The family was getting desperate. Luckily, the family had relatives in Spain, and they had contacted some of the agents who worked for the powerhouse Barcelona team. Barcelona is a major city in Spain. These teams have youth academies that serve as minor leagues and training facilities for young players.

After Barcelona won the Copa del Rey in 2009, Messi finds himself holding yet another trophy. Every year, Messi finds ways to lead Barcelona to more championships.

They were always looking for talent. So Barcelona invited the family to Spain where the coaches were to give Messi a tryout.

They were immediately impressed. Even though he was smaller and younger than the other players, Messi was the fastest. In addition, he handled the ball better than anyone else on the pitch. He scored goal after goal during practice games. There was no doubt that the Barcelona Youth Academy wanted Messi, even though they usually did not take kids as young as he was.

The team doctors gave him a full medical examination and decided that with proper treatment—growth

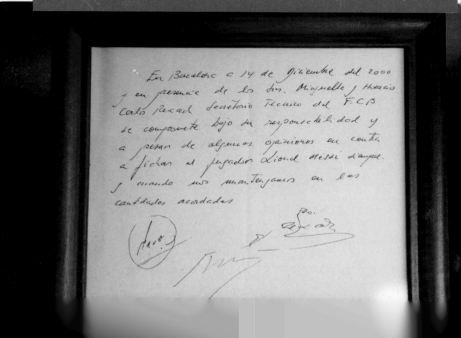

At the age of thirteen, Messi signed his first of many contracts with FC Barcelona. This one is extremely rare because it was signed on a napkin.

hormone injections—Messi would be able to grow to reach almost average height. But there was one more concern they wanted to address before they offered the teenager a contract.

They were worried that he would not be able to handle living so far away from his family. They wanted to put the boy through a series of psychological tests to see how he would hold up.

But Messi's father, at dinner with the academy's sporting director, told the man that he would take Messi home on the very next plane if he wasn't signed immediately to a contract.

The sporting director, Carlos Rexach, instantly grabbed a pen and drew up a makeshift contract on a restaurant napkin. Barcelona would not only train and educate Messi, but they would also pay for all of his medical expenses.

Messi was now a member of Barcelona!

Barcelona!

From 2000 to 2003, Messi played and starred for some of Barcelona's junior teams, gradually making his way up to the Cadete A team. This was basically the highest level of junior team. The level of play, opponent, or age groups never seemed to matter to Messi. On the pitch he was a cool, quick-attacking scoring machine.

Playing with the Cadete A team, he scored an incredible 37 goals in 30 matches!

Even though he was still very young, it was difficult to keep such a talented player from advancing through the ranks. The 2003–04 season was a breakout season of sorts for Messi. He played on five different teams that

After Barcelona signed the young superstar Neymar to team up with Messi, the already dominating Barcelona squad became the most powerful team in the world.

When Messi came on as a substitute in the 2006 World Cup, he became the youngest player ever to represent Argentina at a World Cup.

year, moving his way up to the big club—FC Barcelona, nicknamed "Barca."

On November 16, 2003, Messi—who was only sixteen years old at the time—played his first game for the Barcelona team. It was a friendly match against FC Porto, the name of a team from nearby Portugal. In soccer there are two types of matches: friendly matches, or exhibitions, and official games. Even though the game was a "friendly," the experience was great for Messi as he became the youngest player ever to take the field for Barcelona.

Nearly a year later, in October 2004, there were many Barcelona players sidelined by injury. The club activated Messi for his first official match against RCD Espanyol. Messi played well and would soon find himself activated for just about all the club's official matches.

The following May, Messi became the youngest player ever to register a goal for Barca, when he scored in a game against Albacete. At the time, Messi was only seventeen years, ten months and seven days old.

After receiving his gold medal at the 2008 Olympics in Beijing with Argentina's national team, Messi walks around the track and waves to the full stadium.

Messi obtained his Spanish citizenship, making him a citizen of Spain as well as Argentina. Once he was a Spanish citizen, the country's national team had hoped that he would represent Spain during international competition. They especially wanted him for the World Cup, a tournament held once every four years.

But even though Messi lived in Spain and is forever grateful for what Barca has done for him, he always stayed loyal to his native country. He chose to play for Argentina. So, between games for Barca, Messi also played games for Argentina's U-20 (players less than twenty years old) national team. In 2004, he played international games against other South American national teams from Uruguay and Paraguay. He scored three goals in the two games and was making a name for himself on the international soccer scene.

There appeared to be little doubt that Messi would be chosen to play on Argentina's 2006 World Cup team. He was getting better and better and by the 2005–06 season was a star reserve for Barca. He was off to another great season, scoring 6 goals in 17 games. But he tore a muscle in his leg that March, only months before the World Cup.

No one his age had ever played for Argentina's national team. But the decision was made to add him to the team even though he was not at full strength because of the injury. He did not play during the team's first World Cup match against Ivory Coast, but became the youngest

One of the ways Lionel gives back is through his foundation. He organizes exhibition matches called Messi and Friends where all proceeds from the events are given to charities.

On January 7, 2013, at the age of twenty-five, Messi became the only player ever to win the FIFA Ballon d'Or four times (award was known as Ballon d'Or through 2010).

person ever to play for Argentina when he came on in the next game against Serbia and Montenegro.

He wasn't intimidated at all. He entered the game with about 20 minutes left and immediately set up teammate Hernán Crespo with a beautiful pass that allowed Crespo to score. Then with a few minutes left in the match, Messi scored a goal, making him the youngest player to score during the 2006 World Cup.

The experience of international play made Messi an even stronger player, and he became a starter for Barca during the 2006–07 season. He scored 14 goals despite missing a few months with a broken arm.

During this period, Messi started being compared to a former great Argentinean player—Diego Maradona. This was due in part to his flashy ballhandling skills and electric goals. One game, for example, during an annual tournament known as "El Clásico," Messi scored three goals—a hat trick—to give Barcelona a 3–3 tie. Barcelona was forced to play the game with only ten players instead of eleven, and yet Messi kept tying the score 1–1, 2–2 and finally 3–3 with his tallies.

Messi, who was still a very young player, continued getting better. In 2007–08, he was nominated to be chosen as Soccer's Player of the Year. In addition, he came in third place in the voting for the highest honor in soccer: the Ballon d'Or. But it would not be long before Messi would have to make space in his home for a collection of Ballon d'Or trophies.

The 2008–09 season was one where Messi finally stayed healthy enough to play all season long. It was a breakout campaign for a player already regarded as one of the best in the world.

He played 51 games and scored 38 goals while leading Barca to a season no one would forget. It was the first time a team from Spain had won all three important championships in the same year. Barcelona took home the Copa del Rey, La Liga, and the Champions League titles. During that season, Messi proved that he was more than just a great scorer. He also had 18 assists. This meant that 18 of his passes led directly to one of his teammates scoring a goal.

Believe it or not, for Messi, the best was yet to come.

International Superstar

Lionel Messi has proven over the years that there is nothing on the soccer pitch that is out of his reach. When the Argentinean superstar sets his mind to it, it's as if he plays the game on a certain level that others spend their entire lives trying to reach.

Many, if not all, of the major soccer announcers in the United States, Europe, and South America have called Messi the best soccer player they have ever seen.

In 2008, Messi left Barca for a while—after some tough negotiations—to play for Argentina in the Olympics held in Beijing, China. What did he do? He scored a couple of goals, assisted on a few more, and led Argentina to the

After winning his record-breaking fourth straight Ballon d'Or in 2013, Messi shows off his trophies to the Barcelona fans.

gold medal. Along the way, Argentina defeated soccer powerhouse and rival, Brazil, 3–0.

He took to the world stage again two years later when he played in his second World Cup tournament for Argentina. This time he was coached by the player he is most compared with: Diego Maradona. It was his former idol who decided to move Messi from striker to midfielder for the World Cup. His thinking was that Messi's ballhandling and passing prowess would help the other players score goals.

It worked … almost.

Argentina cruised to victories over Nigeria, Korea Republic (South Korea), and Greece, a game that saw Messi voted the "Man of the Match." Argentina advanced to the next round and defeated a very strong Mexican team 3–1 to make it to the quarterfinals. But Argentina lost to Germany 4–0. Some people questioned whether Maradona should have left Messi at striker.

If he is healthy, Messi will likely be back in the World Cup in 2014.

For now, he continues to dominate the Spanish Premier League and European play as he shatters records and dominates highlight reels. He was the league's top scorer in 2009–10, scoring 34 goals.

He scored a whopping 53 goals the following year and won his third Ballon d'Or trophy.

On March 7, 2012, Messi scored five goals in a single match. A few weeks later, on March 20, 2012, Messi forever entered his name into the Barcelona record books when he scored a hat trick—three goals in a match—to become the all-time leading scorer for Barcelona.

He was not done breaking records.

Later that spring, Messi went on a scoring spree, scoring three goals on May 2 and four goals on May 5. This raised his season scoring total to 72 goals. He finished the season with 73 scores. No one in all of Europe had ever scored so many goals in one season. The previous record, set in 1973, was 67 goals.

Messi keeps very close contact with his old teammates from Argentina, as well as his family and friends. He calls or texts home every day and visits whenever he has time off from the Barcelona team.

In November 2012, Messi became a father for the first time when his son, Thiago, was born. The boy's mother, Antonella Roccuzzo, has been Messi's girlfriend for a long time.

Lionel Messi is clearly a special player, a once in a lifetime soccer talent. But he has never forgotten the hardships he had to go through, the medical problems he endured. With that in mind, in 2007 he started the Leo Messi Foundation.

The charity helps needy children. But one important aspect is that it offers sick children in Argentina the chance to get medical treatment in Spain. Messi's charity pays for the medicine, the travel to Spain, hospital fees, and even a temporary place to live in Spain while the children are being treated.

If it had not been for the Barcelona soccer team willing to pay for Messi's own medical treatment, the world would never have seen such a great soccer player.

In 2010, Messi became a goodwill ambassador for UNICEF, a worldwide organization that stands up for children's rights.

Messi also never forgot where he got his first start in soccer. He paid for the construction of a new dormitory and gymnasium for the Newell's soccer club.

As Lionel Messi began the 2012–13 soccer season as an international superstar for Barcelona, it's almost scary to think that he can get even better and score even more goals. But as the season started Messi was only twenty-five

A lot of times, Messi's foundation will organize exhibition matches that will benefit other organizations in addition to his own.

years old, meaning he will be scoring goals and breaking records for years to come. By comparison, Maradona, the player most people compare Messi with, played professional soccer until he was thirty-seven years old!

Barcelona fans can rest easy that Messi has no intention of ever wearing any other team's jersey.

"I am, and always will be grateful to Barcelona for what they did for me and my family," Messi said in a documentary of his career. "But I play for and fight for the Barcelona shirt because that's how I feel. The club has been a part of me since a young age. I give my all because I don't like to lose and try to give every bit of me for the club and my teammates."

Career Highlights and Awards

- UEFA Champions League Top Goalscorer: 2008–09, 2009–10, 2010–11, 2011–12

- FIFA World Player of the Year: 2009 (renamed FIFA Ballon d'Or after 2009)

- Marca Leyenda Award: 2009

- *World Soccer* Player of the Year: 2009, 2011, 2012

- Onze d'Or: 2009, 2011, 2012

- UEFA Club Footballer of the Year: 2009 (renamed UEFA Best Player in Europe Award)

- Ballon d'Or: 2009 (renamed FIFA Ballon d'Or after 2009)

- FIFA Club World Cup Golden Ball: 2009, 2011

- European Golden Shoe: 2009–10, 2011–12, 2012–13

- FIFA Ballon d'Or: 2010, 2011, 2012

- Copa del Rey Top Goalscorer: 2010–11

- UEFA Best Player in Europe Award: 2011

- Pichichi Trophy: 2009–10, 2011–12, 2012–13

- La Liga Champion: 2004–05, 2005–06, 2008–09, 2009–10, 2010–11, 2012–13

- UEFA Champions League Champion: 2005–06, 2008–09, 2010–11

- Supercopa de España Champion: 2005, 2006, 2009, 2010, 2011

- Copa del Rey Champion: 2008–09, 2011–12

- UEFA Super Cup Champion: 2009, 2011

- Only player to ever win four Ballon d'Or awards.

- Scored his 300th career goal with Barcelona on February 16, 2013.

- Won the ESPY award for Best International Athlete in 2012.

- Won an Olympic Gold Medal with Argentina in 2008.

- Only player to win the Ballon d'Or, FIFA World Player, Pichichi trophy, and Golden Boot in same season: 2009–10.

INTERNET ADDRESSES

Unofficial Fan Page of Lionel Messi
<http://messi.com/>

Official FC Barcelona Web Site
<http://www.fcbarcelona.com/>

FIFA Official Site
<http://www.fifa.com/>

Harris County Public Library
Houston, Texas

INDEX